This doodle book belongs to:

_____

The Pocket Bible Doodle Book

ZONDERkidz

ZONDERVAN.com/
AUTHORTRACKER
follow your favorite authors

ZONDERKIDZ
The Pocket Bible Doodle Book
Copyright © 2011 by Bookworks LLC

Requests for information should be addressed to:
Zonderkidz, *Grand Rapids, Michigan 49530*

[in Blue only:] ISBN 978-0-310-72834-4
[in Green only:] ISBN 978-0-310-72835-1

Cover Design: Sarah Molegraaf
Illustrations: © 2011 Brian Oesch

Printed in China

11 12 13 14 15 16 /SCC/ 17 16 15 14 13 12 11 10 9 8 7 6 5 4 3 2 1

Our story starts with only one being, and it was God. There was only darkness until he separated darkness from light on the first day. On day two, he separated water in the sky from water in the air. Draw clouds, rivers, and lakes to finish this scene.

God created plants and trees on the third day.
Design your own plant.

Create your own tree.

Fill this garden with flowers.

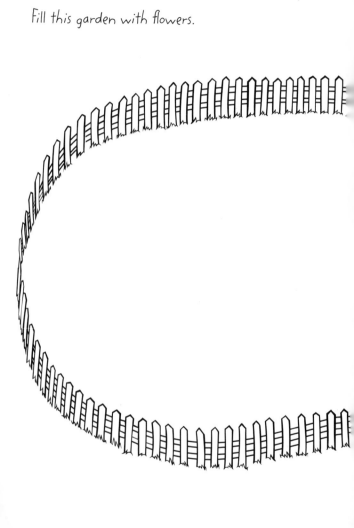

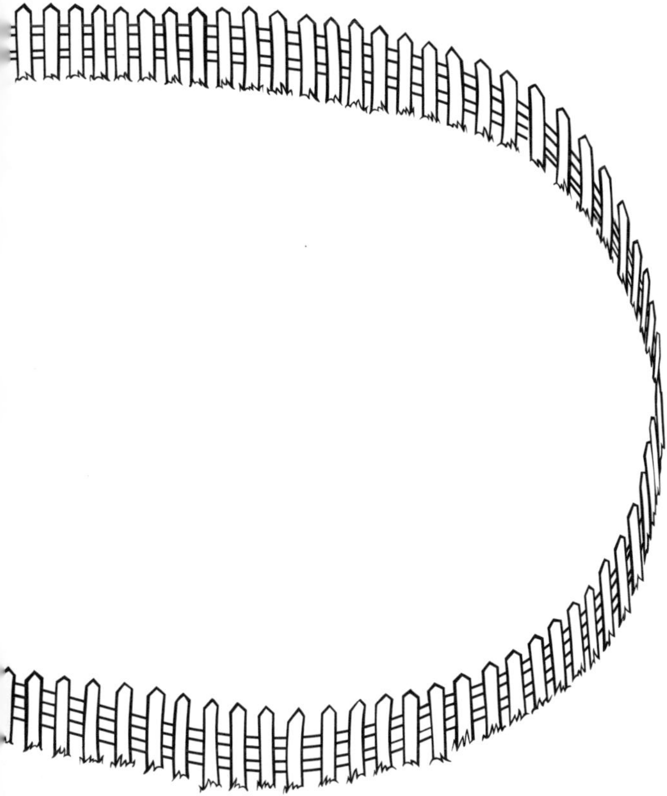

God created the great creatures of the sea on the fifth day. Create your own sea creatures.

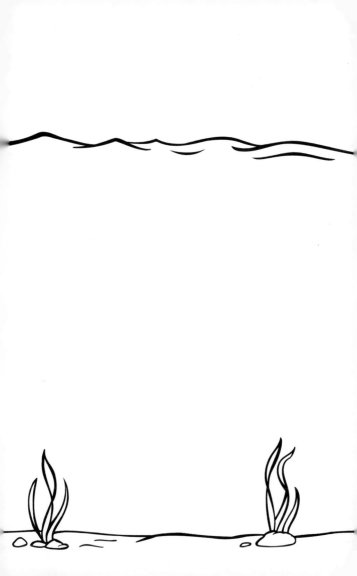

God created birds of the air on the fifth day.
Draw your own birds.

Give this turtle a special shell design.

Fill this nest.

God created wild animals on the sixth day.

Create your own wild animals.

Complete this dog's face.

Finish this drawing.

What lives here?

Finish this drawing.

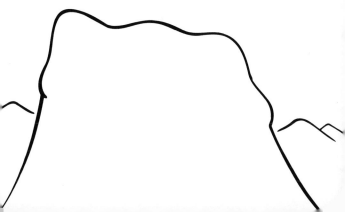

God created Adam on the sixth day.
Finish this drawing.

Draw the fruit that may have grown on the Tree of Knowledge of Good and Evil.

Adam named all the animals, including the spider. Design your own spider web.

Draw a furry friend.

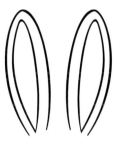

After Adam and Eve sinned, God placed angels and a flaming sword at the Garden of Eden's entrance. Finish this scene.

You are made in the likeness of God.
Draw a picture of yourself.

Draw your family here.

Noah built the ark. What do you think it looked like?

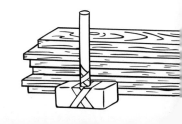

Noah had to take at least two of every animal with him. What animals would you be sure to gather?

Noah had to pack every kind of food that was to be eaten. Fill these baskets and plates.

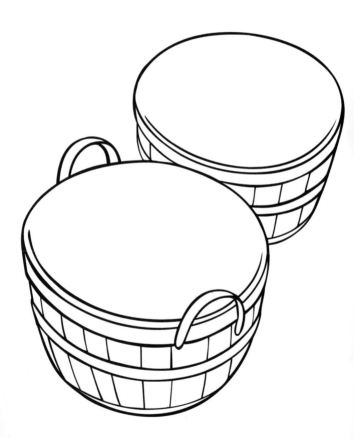

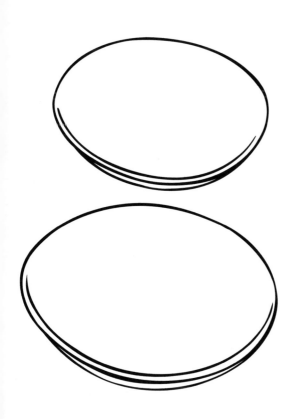

God blessed Abram for following his word.
Finish this drawing.

Baby Isaac was the promised child of Abraham. Finish this drawing.

Rebekah became Isaac's wife after watering a servant's camel. Finish this drawing.

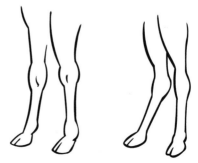

The servant brought clothing and jewelry to
Rebekah and her family. Finish this drawing.

Rebekah moved from her father's land to marry Isaac. What animals filled her father's land?

Jacob dreamed of a stairway to heaven.
Draw it here.

Jacob met Rachel, a shepherdess, at a well.
Draw her sheep here.

God changed Jacob's name to Israel.
Write your name here and draw things
that represent who you are.

Finish the pattern on Joseph's coat of many colors.

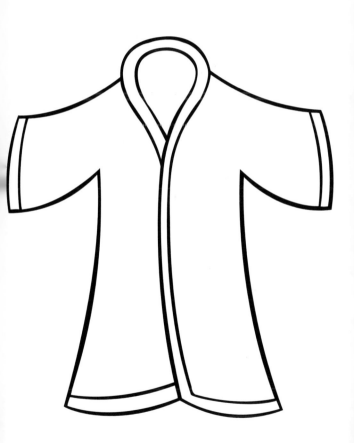

Joseph dreamed that sheaves of grain bowed down to his sheaf. Finish this drawing.

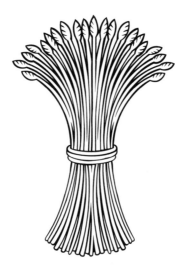

Joseph dreamed that the sun, moon, and eleven stars bowed down to him. Finish this drawing.

Joseph was sold to a caravan of merchants. What were they carrying on their camels?

While in prison with Joseph, the cupbearer dreamed of himself handing a cup to Pharaoh. Finish the drawing of this dream.

The chief baker dreamed of birds eating from three baskets of bread on his head. Finish the drawing of this dream.

Pharaoh dreamed of seven fat cows and seven skinny cows, then seven full heads of wheat and seven thin heads of wheat. Finish the drawing of this dream.

Joseph's silver cup was found in Benjamin's sack of grain. Complete the drawing.

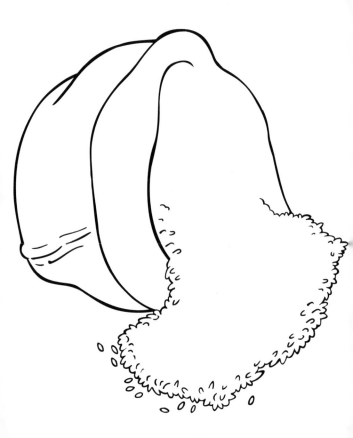

Instead of traveling with a sack of grain,
you might travel with a suitcase.
Design your own suitcase here.

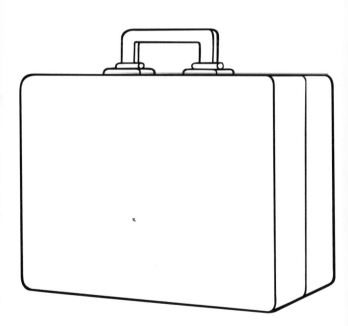

Joseph went to meet his father in a chariot.
What do you think the chariot looked like?

Cars have replaced chariots. Design your own four-wheeled hot rod.

Moses floated on the Nile River in a small basket until the princess found him. Draw baby Moses.

God spoke to Moses though a burning bush.
Finish the scene.

Moses took his staff with him when he went to
see Pharoah. Complete the scene.

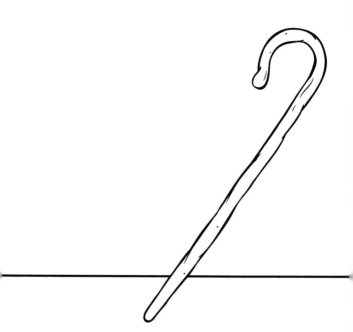

God sent ten plagues.

Plague number one: The water of the Nile River turned to blood. Complete the scene.

Plague number two: Frogs covered the land.
Complete the scene.

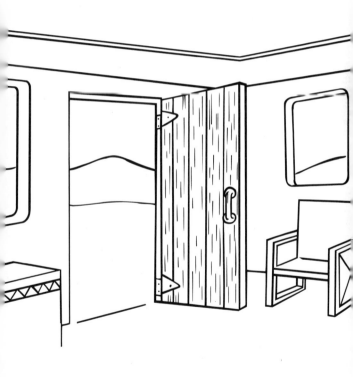

Plague number three: Gnats came upon men and animals. Complete the scene.

Plague number four: Houses were filled with swarms of flies. Complete the scene.

Plague number five: Sickness became widespread among the livestock. Complete the scene.

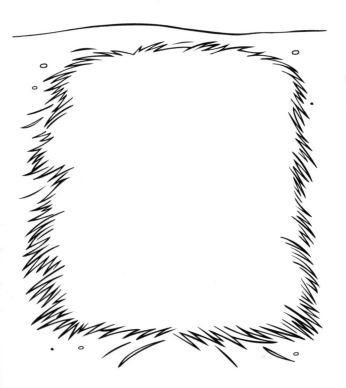

Plague number six: Boils appeared on men and animals. Complete the scene.

Plague number seven: Hail fell upon the land.
Complete the scene.

Plague number eight: Locusts devoured every tree that grew in the field. Complete the scene.

Plague number nine: Darkness filled the land. If darkness filled your bedroom, what would you use for light?

Plague number ten: Every firstborn son in Egypt died. Then Pharaoh said, "Go!" Each Israelite man had his cloak tucked into his belt, his sandals on, and his staff in hand.
Complete this drawing.

With God's help, Moses parted the Red Sea. Finish this scene.

After the Egyptian army was swallowed up in the Red Sea, Miriam and the women sang and danced. Complete this drawing.

God sent manna and quail to the Israelites.

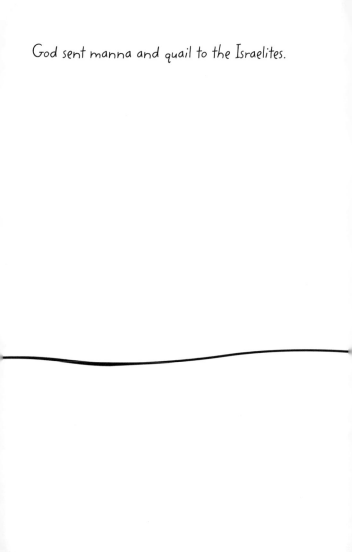

When Moses struck the rock, water gushed
from it. Add your own gushing water.

God lead the Israelites with a pillar of fire and pillar of cloud. Doodle those two things here.

God spoke to Moses on Mount Sinai. It was covered with a thick cloud and surrounded with thunder and lightning. Finish this scene.

God gave Moses the Ten Commandments.
Doodle an image for each commandment
(Exodus 20).

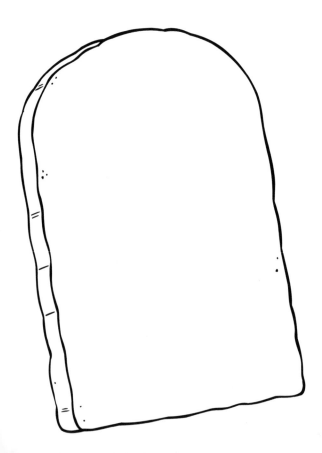

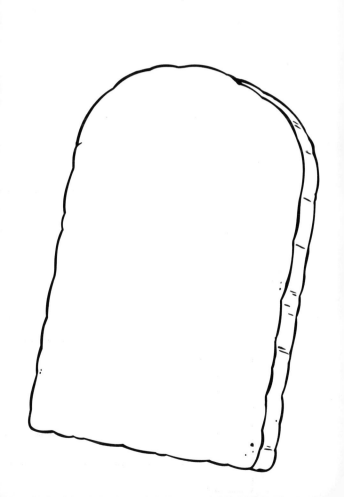

Decorate the ark of the covenant (Exodus 25).

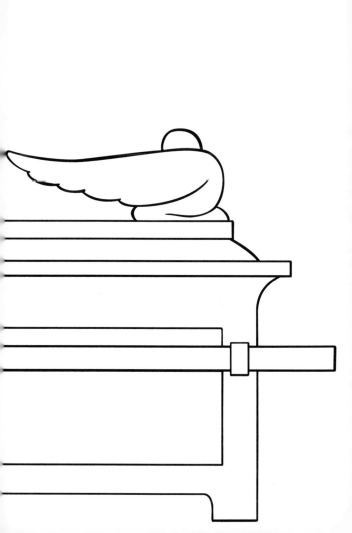

Draw the table and lampstand found in the tabernacle (Exodus 25).

Before Moses came down from Mount Sinai, the Israelites crafted a golden calf. What do you think it looked like?

Spies were sent to the land of Canaan. The land flowed with milk and honey and offered great fruit. What fruits do you love to eat?

Balaam's donkey saw an angel of the Lord that Balaam could not see. Complete this scene.

The walls of Jericho fell when seven priests blew their trumpets and the Israelites shouted. Complete this scene.

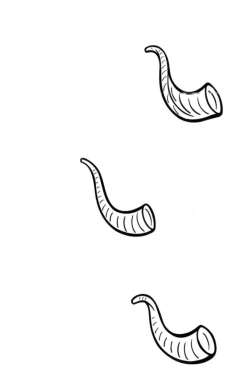

Deborah led Israel and settled arguments under the Palm of Deborah. Add her to this scene.

Gideon won a battle with 300 men, torches, trumpets, and empty jars. Can you draw those things here?

God promised Samson strength as long as he didn't cut his hair. Finish the drawing.

Samson was given strength one last time so that he could push down the pillars.
Complete this scene.

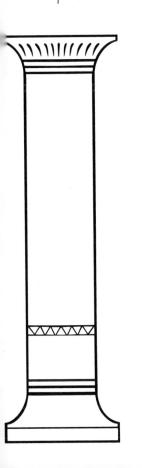
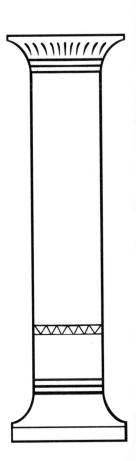

Ruth and Naomi were best friends.
Draw yourself and one of your best friends.

When Samuel was asleep, God spoke to him.
Finish this scene.

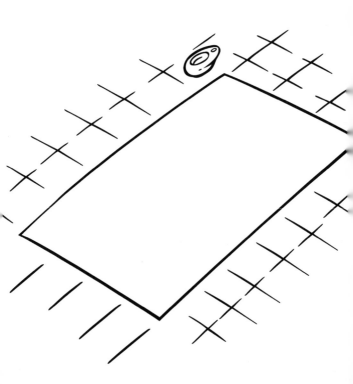

What does your bedroom look like?

Saul became the first king of Israel, anointed by Samuel. Complete the drawing.

If you were king or queen of Israel, what would you look like?

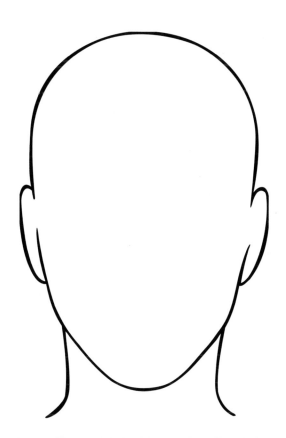

When Saul became king, the Israelites had a great feast and celebration. Decorate the scene.

After David was anointed by Samuel to be the next king, David played the harp for King Saul. Complete this drawing.

What instrument would you play for a king?

Use these lines to create the coat of armor, sword, and helmet King Saul thought David should use against Goliath.

Goliath towered over David, but David was the victor. Complete this drawing.

King David wrote many songs to honor God.
Can you write one psalm here?

Write your own song or poem to the Lord.

King Solomon built a temple for the Lord in Jerusalem. Use these doodles to create your own temple.

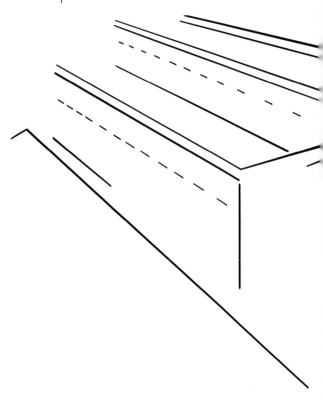

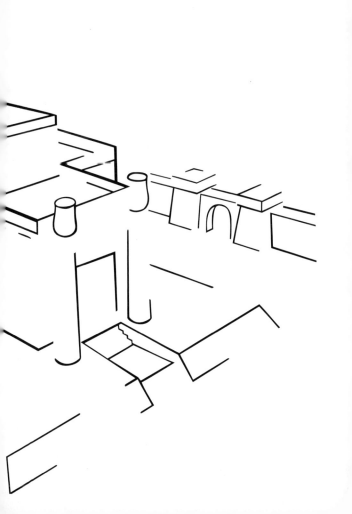

Solomon decorated the temple with gourds and flowers. Design your own decorations.

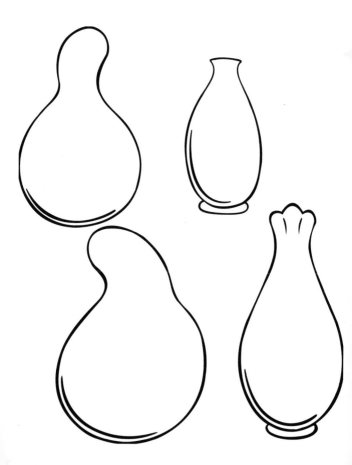

Solomon covered the inside of the temple with gold. Imagine the hallways in the temple and fill in this scene.

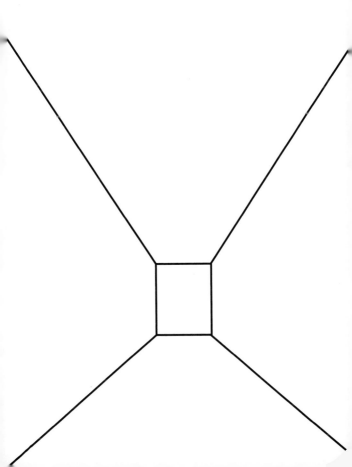

There was an inner sanctuary at the temple where Solomon placed statues of angels. Create your own statue here.

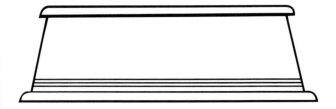

Heavy doors carved with angels, palm trees, and flowers stood at the entrance to the sanctuary. What do you think they looked like?

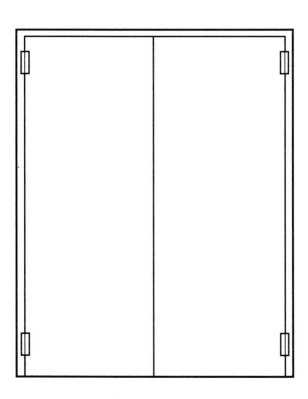

In the temple was a golden altar, the golden table, lampstands of pure gold, and dishes of pure gold. Draw some of these things.

Solomon was wise and taught about animals and
birds. Draw some here.

Solomon taught about reptiles. Finish this scene.

Solomon taught about fish. Fill the bowl.

Who's looking at you?

Complete this magnificent bird.

It took Solomon thirteen years to build his palace. Finish this palace.

Solomon decorated his palace with many flowers and plants. Fill this pot.

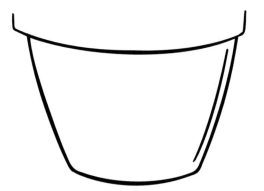

Water was plentiful. Design your own water pattern shooting from this modern sprinkler.

The queen of Sheba visited Solomon. She brought a very large caravan. Imagine what that looked like and finish the scene.

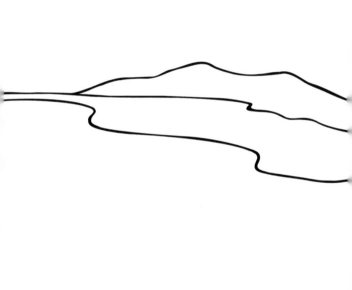

What do you think the queen of Sheba looked like?

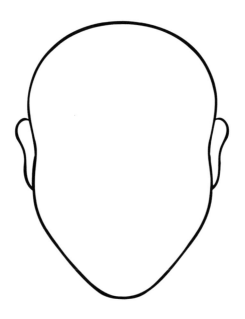

Design the queen of Sheba's beautiful slippers.

The queen brought large quantities of precious stones and spices. Finish this drawing.

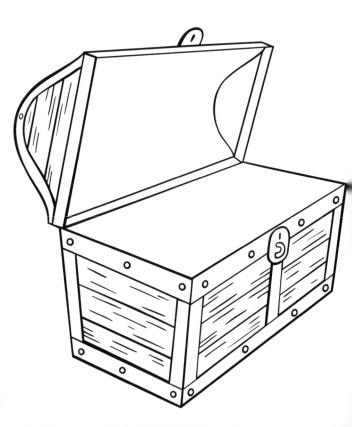

The queen brought King Solomon wood for making instruments. Create your own wooden instrument.

Ships came from foreign places, bringing gifts
for King Solomon. Draw your ship here.

Elijah was a prophet of God. He was fed by ravens and drank from a brook.
Finish this scene.

Elijah prepared the altar for God and even
poured four large jars of water on the altar and
the wood. Elijah prayed to God, and the Lord
responded by sending fire to burn up the wood,
the stones, the bull, and the soil.
Finish this scene.

What can you give to God as a sacrifice?

Elijah was taken up to heaven in a chariot of fire drawn by horses of fire. Imagine the scene and draw it here.

Elisha took twenty loaves of barley bread and fed 100 hungry men. Draw your own bread.

What's your favorite meal?

Naaman was the commander of the army and a valiant soldier. Complete this drawing.

Naaman was healed of his leprosy after washing in the Jordan River. Finish this scene.

Thankfully you don't have to bathe in a river.
Design your own shower curtain.

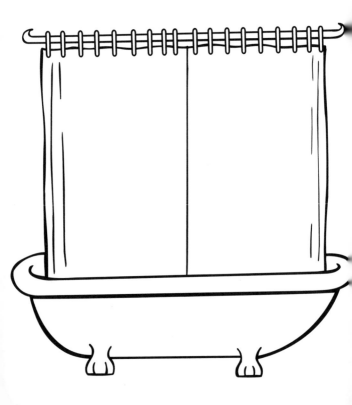

If you could design your own towel, what would it look like?

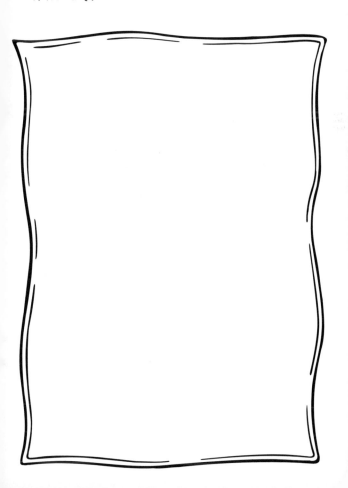

There were many kings who ruled over Israel.
Finish designing these crowns.

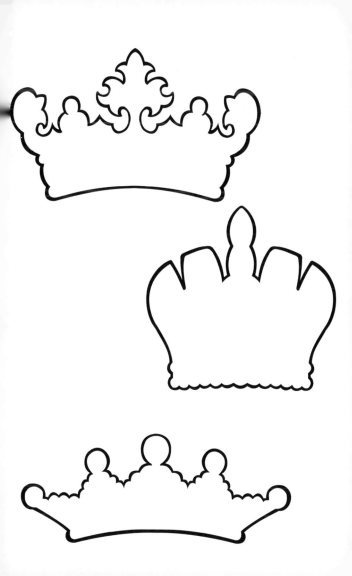

Kings came in all different sizes.
Finish this drawing.

Some kings followed God, and some did not.
Finish this drawing.

Old Testament soldiers used bows and arrows.
Design your own bow and arrows.

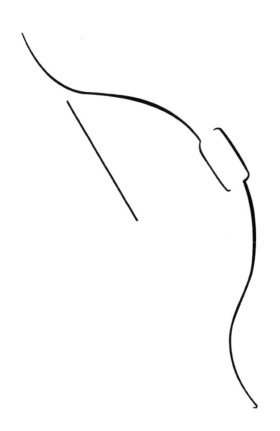

Trumpets were used at the temple.
Design your own trumpet flag.

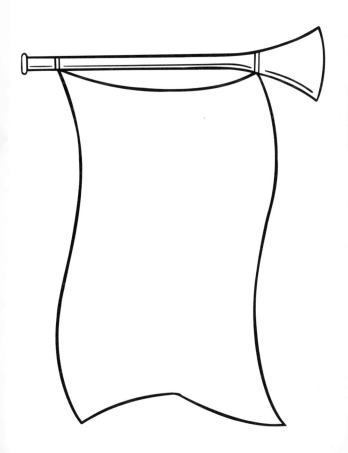

Maps helped show boundaries between
kingdoms. Draw a map of your neighborhood.

Prophets traveled from town to town. If you were a prophet, what would your tent look like?

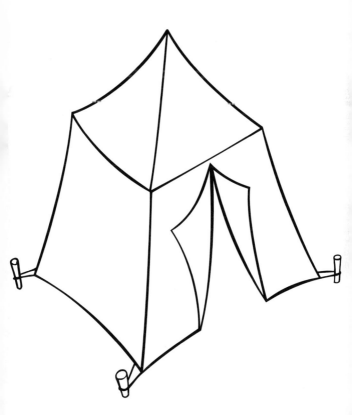

Soldiers kept watch over Jerusalem.
Draw the soldiers that would be
keeping watch in this scene.

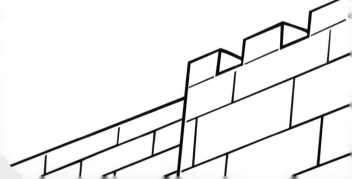

Josiah became king when he was eight years old. Decorate this cake for his birthday.

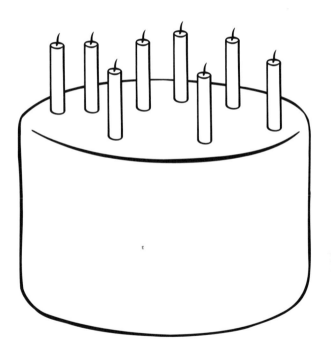

King Josiah was a good king, fair in all of his measurements and decisions. What would you weigh on this scale?

Josiah burned the idols outside of Jerusalem's city gates. Design your own gates here.

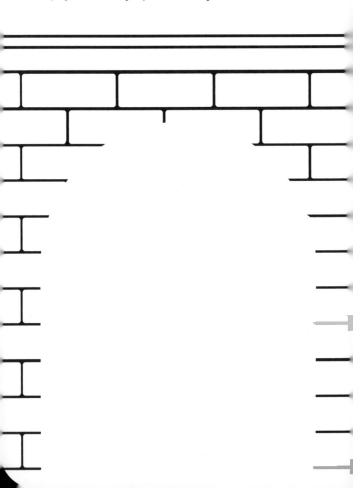

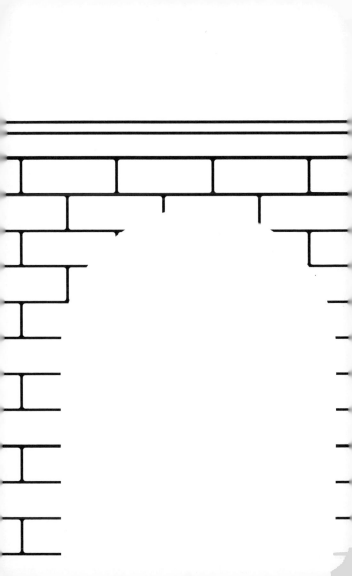

Let the fields be jubilant!

The trees of the forest will sing.

There were many jobs at the temple. This man is a priest in charge of purifying the holy things.

This man is a priest assigned to baking the holy bread.

This man is a gatekeeper.

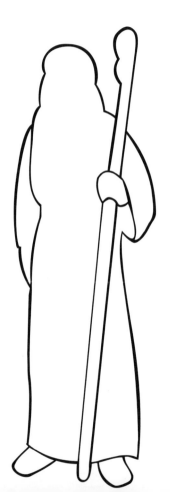

This man is one of the many singers.

Couriers used horses to deliver messages throughout the kingdom. Draw your own horses here.

After years of exile, the Israelites returned to Jerusalem. They had to rebuild. Finish this drawing by adding the Sheep Gate.

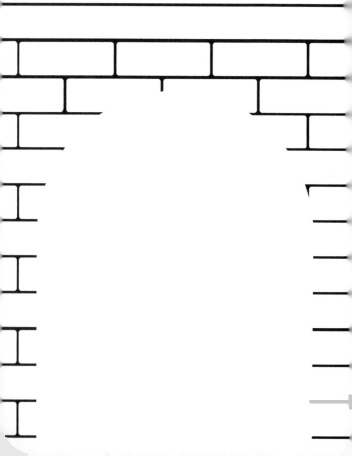

Finish this drawing by adding the Fish Gate.

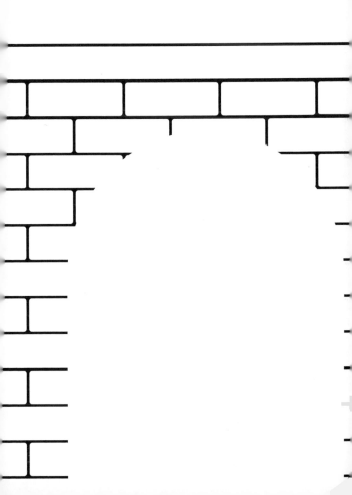

When the Israelites returned to Jerusalem, they celebrated by eating some of the finest food. Create an ice-cream sundae in this bowl.

Create your favorite pizza on this platter.

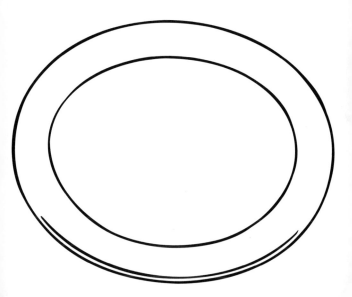

Esther was lovely, and she won favor with King Xerxes. Finish this drawing.

Design a robe that Queen Esther
may have worn.

Complete this crown, fit for a queen.

When Queen Esther went to King Xerxes to make her request, he held out the gold scepter that was in his hand. Finish this scepter.

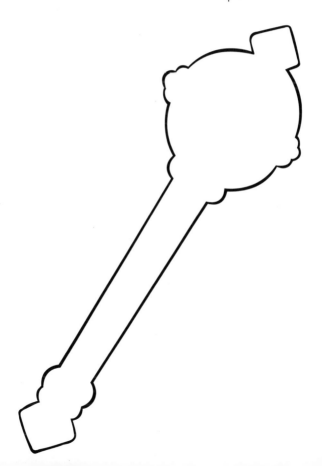

Shadrach, Meshach, and Abednego were thrown into a fiery furnace because they refused to bow down to false gods. Finish this scene ... and don't forget to add the angel of the Lord!

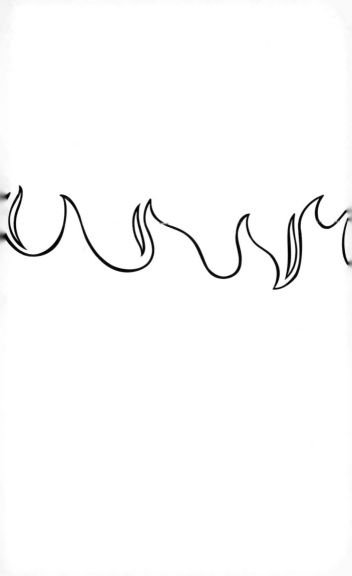

Daniel was put into a lions' den because he prayed to God instead of King Darius. Finish this scene.

Daniel had a vision of God. Draw this scene:

The Ancient of Days took his seat. His clothing was as white as snow; the hair of his head was white like wool. His throne was flaming with fire, and its wheels were all ablaze.

Jonah was told to go to Nineveh. Instead he got on a boat headed to Tarshish. Finish this scene.

Jonah was tossed into the sea and was soon swallowed by a great fish. Finish this scene.

Draw the scene where the fish spit Jonah
onto dry land.

Jesus was born. The promised Messiah had arrived. Finish this scene.

Jesus is the Prince of Peace.

Jesus is the living water. Draw a well to remind you of Jesus' promise that you will never be thirsty again.

Jesus is the Lamb of God. Complete this picture.

Jesus is the Lion of Judah. Finish this drawing.

Jesus is the Bread of Life. Finish this drawing.

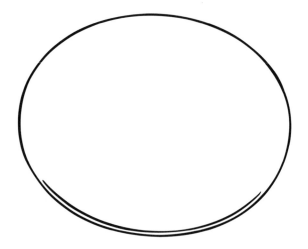

Jesus is the vine. We are the branches.
What grows on this vine?

Jesus is a good shepherd. And we are like sheep. Finish this scene.

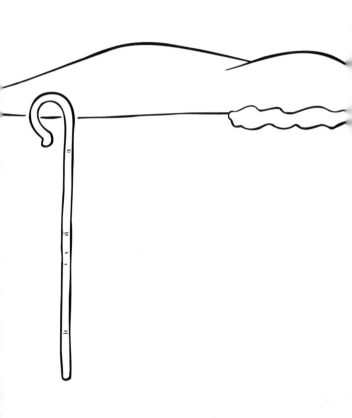

Jesus is the Morningstar. Design your own
Morningstar.

A woman poured perfume on Jesus' feet as a sign of her love for him.
Design this perfume bottle.

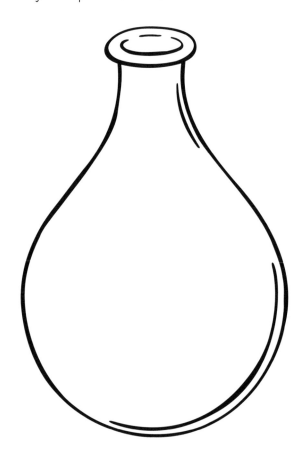

What gift would you give Jesus?

Draw the colt that Jesus rode into Jerusalem.

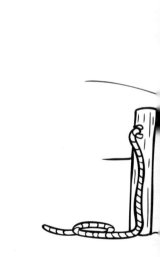

"Hosanna in the highest!"
Fill in these palm branches.

How do you praise Jesus?

Jesus' washed the disciples' feet.

How do you serve others?

What do you think the Upper Room looked like?

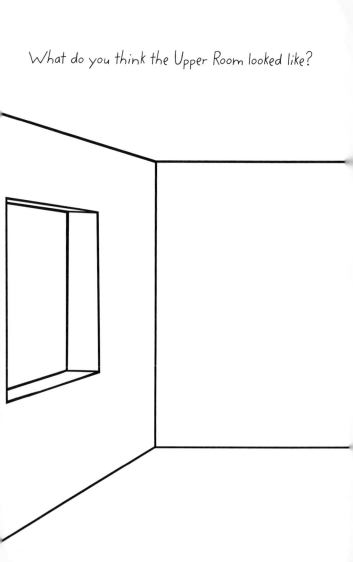

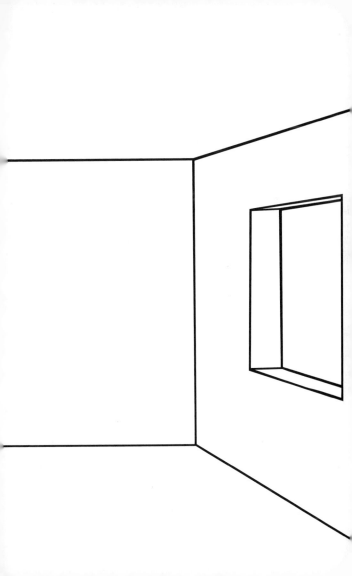

Jesus shared the Last Supper with his disciples.
Fill the table with the food they enjoyed.

Jesus took the bread, gave thanks, broke it,
and gave it to his disciples.

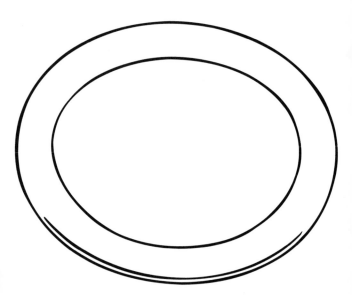

Then he took the cup, gave thanks, and offered it to the disciples.

Before the rooster crowed twice, Peter betrayed Jesus three times. Finish this rooster.

The soldiers placed a crown of thorns upon Jesus' head. What did that crown look like?

Jesus is alive. Finish this scene of Easter morning.

We celebrate Jesus' life and death today. Hallelujah! He is risen! Complete this church scene.

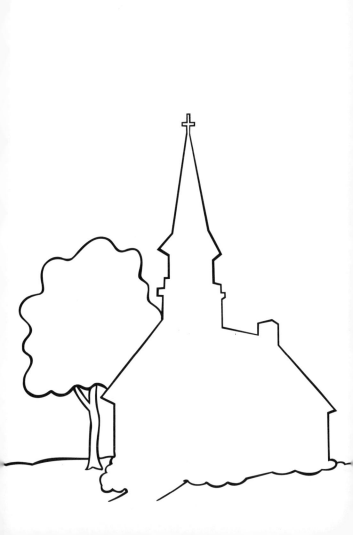

Finish this Easter flower bouquet.

Create a stained glass window.

Jesus ascended into heaven. Finish this scene.

The Holy Spirit came and appeared like tongues of fire. Finish this scene.

Create your own masterpiece.

What does the House of the Lord look like to you?

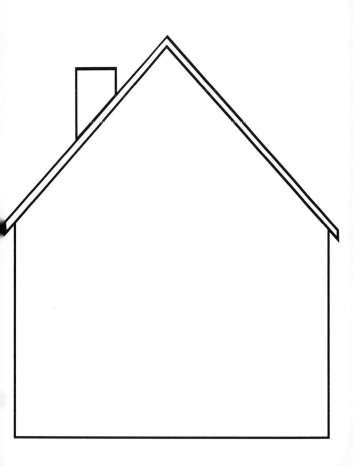

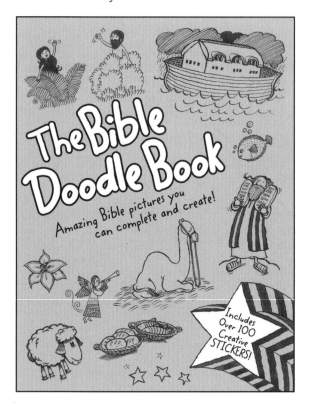